What is Jill wearing?
What is Conor holding?
Who is wearing red pants?

He

This is Jill.

This is Conor.

This is Helen.

2

3

 Hello!

This is Bunny.

This is Rex.

This is Tabby.

4

Bunny

Rex

Tabby

8

q

12

13

Hello!

Conor   Jill   Helen

Tabby   Rex   Bunny

14

Hello! Hello everyone!

Jill

Conor

Helen

Tabby

Rex

Bunny

15